MW01245217

BARON GEISLER

SURRENDER with my hands wide open

PRIMIX
PUBLISHING
THE WRITE CHOICE

Primix Publishing
11620 Wilshire Blvd
Suite 900, West Wilshire Center, Los Angeles, CA, 90025
www.primixpublishing.com
Phone: 1-800-538-5788

© 2022 Baron Geisler. All rights reserved.
Narrated by Maria Niza Mariñas

No part of this book may be reproduced, stored in a retrieval system, or transmitted by any means without the written permission of the author.

Published by Primix Publishing   06/16/2022

ISBN: 978-1-955944-44-1(sc)
ISBN: 978-1-955944-45-8(e)

Library of Congress Control Number: 2021924207

Any people depicted in stock imagery provided by iStock are models, and such images are being used for illustrative purposes only.

Certain stock imagery © iStock.

Because of the dynamic nature of the Internet, any web addresses or links contained in this book may have changed since publication and may no longer be valid. The views expressed in this work are solely those of the author and do not necessarily reflect the views of the publisher, and the publisher hereby disclaims any responsibility for them.

CONTENTS

INTRODUCTION

To movie and TV fans, I am the actor **BARON GEISLER**, who grew up before your eyes. Onscreen, you've seen me in countless roles—the carefree and lovestruck teenager, the conflicted guy with several demons to slay, the director of a reality show on TV, the sidekick of a kingpin, the wayward, repentant son, among many others.

The Child (Anak) is a 2000 Filipino family drama film directed by Rory Quintos starring Vilma Santos and Claudine Barretto, with Joel Torre and Baron Geisler. The film was critically acclaimed by film critics. It was the Philippines' submission to the 73rd Academy Awards for the Academy Award for Best Foreign Language Film.

Still Image from the 2000 film ANAK

In real life, I am simply Baron Frederick Von Geisler—son, brother husband, and father. And above all, a servant of Christ.

I was born on June 5, 1982 at the Clark Air Base Hospital in Pampanga to a German father, Donald David Geisler and a Filipina mother, Gracia Bayonito-Geisler. My dad, a former US serviceman, passed away in 2002 at the age of 69. My mother joined him and our Creator in 2017.

MY PARENTS

I am the youngest of five siblings. The eldest, Maria Angelica Geisler-Nguyen is a doctor based in San Pablo, California, USA. The second, Ana Maria Geisler-Pineda is a dentist. The third one is Donald David Geisler III or Donnie to us, his family, as well as the world of taekwondo, of which he is a bemedaled athlete, having won several golds for the Philippines. The fourth sibling is Grace Gail Geisler-Morales. I am proud of all of them and their achievements. I feel blessed and privileged to be the family's *bunso*.

I also have three half-siblings in the US: two sisters, one of whom sadly passed away already, and a brother, Donald David Geisler II, whose conversations with me via Facebook Messenger I truly enjoy.

Two of the remaining family photos we have since a fire gutted our home several years ago.

GEISLER HOME

I grew up in a home where all our material needs were provided for. We lived a very comfortable life, luxurious by most standards, in fact. We always had imported goods. I loved going grocery shopping with my parents and siblings at the commissary located inside the air base. We would have the Fudge chocolate, popsicles, Baskin-Robbins, Burger King.

Dad and mom made sure we were given

everything we needed. They used to own a general merchandise store that sold refrigerators and TV sets so financially, we were doing much better than the average family.

Our house was located just a few meters away from the main gate of Clark Air Base. Going to Clark was like visiting another country. We were surrounded by nature. There were a lot of flowers and trees.

Like the typical American household, it was our tradition to celebrate Thanksgiving every third week of November. I always associate Thanksgiving with the delicious aroma of food wafting from our kitchen. Our home would smell of cranberry sauce, freshly baked bread and roasted turkey. These smells remind me of a happy home. They bring me back to a time when life was worry-free and I was just a child soaking all the happiness in, wanting it to never end.

I remember my parents hosting parties for their friends. Dad and mom liked entertaining guests at home so every Saturday, Dad would bring his friends from the military to our house and we would all have a feast. It was as if we were celebrating an important occasion every Saturday. Mom had a *bahay kubo* built for Dad which could accommodate around seven couples and they would stay there. Dad had a lot of friends from the military. He fought during the Korean War as part of the 7th Infantry Division. He got bombed and as a result had a bad back.

We were among the first ones to have cable TV so every Saturday, I would watch all the morning cartoons, like Sesame Street. I looked forward to Saturdays because of those shows that made my childhood a happy one.

When Dad would come home from his annual trip to the States, he would bring boxes and boxes of goodies and we would all get excited opening all those packages. Most of the time, it would be a new computer game such as Atari or Nintendo. I loved collecting toys then. I had figures of G.I. Joe, Teenage Mutant Ninja Turtles, Star Wars, Star Trek, and ships. Any toy that was popular during those times, name it, we had it.

Dad would also bring different kinds of video cameras so we could make home videos. We lost most of the tapes when our home got burned but I believe my sister kept a copy of a tape that showed how much of a crybaby I was at age five. During Christmas, a friend would come to our house and take photos of us wearing the barong. That was our Christmas tradition.

SIBLING LOVE

With my brother Donnie

Growing up, I was always compared to my brother Donnie, who's three years older than me. We always did things together and up to this day, I look up to him. He is my hero. Being younger, I always wanted to fit into his world and become friends with his friends.

My dad enrolled us both at the Club Gymnastica in Clark. Then, of course, we did taekwondo.

I am the family's baby so they were all gentle to me. Yes, I was the golden child but Donnie was the like the diamond in the sky in their eyes because he excelled in taekwondo, competing and winning in international competitions and bringing honor to the country.

Donnie also played soccer at the Palarong Pambansa. Being raised to be competitive, I felt immense pressure to also make a mark but I knew early on that sports was not for me, no matter how hard I tried or trained. I also sensed favoritism as far as my parents' treatment of us was concerned. We were made aware that if we excelled, we would be treated differently from the rest. And because it was Donnie who did, he was given special treatment. He ate the best food. I remember he even traveled with my dad to South Korea while the rest of us were made to stay in Bicol. Perhaps it was my parents' way of showing that if you are the best at what you do, your reward will be great.

And since I was not good at sports, I had to prove

myself in other areas, such as academics. In school, I received several medals for winning in the quiz bee, math contests, spelling bee, even poster-making contests. I needed to prove to my family, especially to my parents, that I was worth something. That I was also somebody that they could be proud of.

COOL DAD, STRICT MOM

Mom and dad were poles apart but I guess it was also their differences that made their marriage work. Dad had a wicked sense of humor. He loved fooling around with fake farts, ugly shirts from Hawaii, icky novelty items. He was cute that way. And he was such a gentle man. For all my naughty ways, I don't remember him ever spanking me.

My father and I at home

Mom, on the other hand, was fond of knick-knacks and expensive things. We used to have a big table where we placed our gold-plated and silver utensils. She had stacks upon stacks of jewelry catalogues. She designed her own jewelry and clothes. She even sew her own outfits. She was one amazing and talented woman.

My mother and I in the piano

I consider myself a Mama's boy but mom was extremely strict with all of us. When she was mad, we would all get terrified. She had such a strong personality. We depended on her for everything because she was the one who handled the finances. Perhaps we were too young to understand things. Maybe we were just too weak to handle that kind of upbringing. We felt that even if we had everything we needed, we couldn't do things that we wanted to do. We were confused because it was not explained to us why we were disciplined that way. This was the reason why my siblings and I wanted to escape from the house. My eldest sister left for the States and excelled there as a doctor. Donnie also left home at an early age to pursue his career in taekwondo.

But to be fair to Mom, she also had her tender moments, especially when she was in front of my *Lola*. I used to have nightmares. So she would lay my head on her lap every single night and caress my hair until I fell asleep.

As a child, I used to pick fights in school. I'd be in fistfights and make my classmates' nose bleed. Because of my constant misbehavior, my mom would get called to the principal's office at least once or twice a month. The principal would ask who was causing trouble and tell me: *Naku, ikaw pa na mukhang anghel ang nanakit*? But obviously, I was no angel.

I remember punching a classmate just because he had a weird face. Years later, we saw each other at a parking lot in Australia and he wanted to hit me but was stopped because my then girlfriend, who was half-Australian, intervened. I had no idea someone was carrying a grudge against me for years and had long wanted to get back at me because of what I had done when we were still children.

SUPERNATURAL EXPOSURE

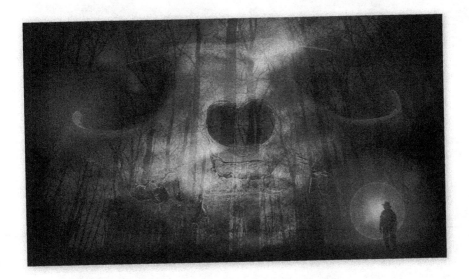

    I was afraid of the dark because we would always watch horror movies. At the age of five, I was already watching films such as Hellraiser 1 and 2. They'd give me nightmares. We were also a family that believed in mythical creatures such as the *manananggal* and *kapre*. TV shows like The Teen Wolf were very popular then. Even back then, I was already fascinated with wolves and vampires. I would go up the roof, pray to Jesus and tell Him: There's going to be a full moon tomorrow. Please turn me into a wolf or a vampire. This fascination for such creatures I carried with me as I was growing up.

Unlike most kids my age, my childhood heroes were the not the usual superheroes like Superman. My heroes were the monsters.

We also practiced *santigwar*, a healing ritual among the Bicolanos. My *lola* was a *spiritista* so whenever we got sick, she and my mom would perform the *santigwar* on us. We were told that it was a way to find out if our sickness was inflicted on us by a person or a bad spirit. Then we would pray so that we would be healed. When I became a Christian later on in my adult life, I found out that what we practiced was witchcraft.

ROAD TO STARDOM

Joining showbiz was not a dream of mine at the start. As a kid, I wanted to be a banker or veterinarian, the regular "dream" jobs of children my age during those years. But as a kid, I was fond of staying alone in my room. I'd sit in front of the TV and watch movies such as Summer Class. I guess that's how my fascination for the world of entertainment started.

With my co-stars at Ang TV

And then when I turned 12, God led me to a totally different path without me knowing it. The popular ABS-CBN kiddie variety show, "Ang TV" which featured several child stars and launched the career of countless actors and actresses, had a show and held auditions for newbies in Pampanga.

I went with my brother, Donnie and his friend just to see what the fuss was about. While there, I was amazed at the adulation being thrown at Patrick Garcia's way. Why are all these girls screaming at him and calling his name? I asked myself. I was fascinated. I wanted that same kind of admiration for myself, too. Little did I know that that harmless moment would be a turning point in my life, showbiz became instantly attractive to my young mind. The world of entertainment beckoned and I was all too willing to say yes.

I gave it a go and auditioned. My brother Donnie and his friend signed my name on the audition sheet. I had no talent in singing and dancing but I sang and danced, anyway. For me, it was just child's play and I had nothing to lose. If I'd get accepted, I'd be happy. If I got turned down, then it's not meant for me. But as luck would have it, I was picked from among more than 800 kids who were screened. And from then, I embraced the industry I had proudly become part of, warts and all.

My parents initially didn't want me to join showbiz but I pleaded and cried to them so they finally relented. But pursuing showbiz at an early age so that I could get away from home for a while meant going through certain inconveniences. I remember having to wake up as early as 3 a.m. for our 7 a.m. calltime at ABS-CBN. And even if our family had two cars, my mom would not let me use them. I had to take the bus with my sister, Angel and an aunt so I could go to Manila from Pampanga. Despite the hardship, I was already enjoying what I was doing at that age and admittedly, it was also an excuse to get away from a home whose rules I felt were stifling me.

After my stint with Ang TV, I was signed up as a member of ABS-CBN's Star Circle Batch 5, an elite group of promising and young actors and actresses being groomed for stardom. I also became part of an all-male trio called Koolits, which included my batchmates John Lloyd Cruz and Marc Solis. Just three regular guys having fun at work and getting paid for it.

With my co-stars at Koolits, Marc Solis and John Lloyd Cruz.

More showbiz offers came in and in 1996, I was cast in the youth-oriented program, Gimik, which was topbilled by Judy Ann Santos, the late Rico Yan, Diether Ocampo, Jolina Magdangal, and Marvin Agustin, among many others. In 1999, I got one of my most memorable roles to date and the character most TV viewers from that generation will always associate me with—the funny and fun-loving Fonzy of the hit afternoon youth drama, Tabing Ilog. Touted as Philippine showbiz's version of the popular American series Dawson's Creek, it starred John Lloyd Cruz, Kaye Abad, Jodi Sta. Maria, Patrick Garcia, Desiree del Valle, Paolo Contis, Paula Peralejo and myself. It was such a hit among the young because it mirrored the joys and pains of growing up.

With the cast of Tabing Ilog

Earning my own money at such a young age gave me the confidence boost I needed. At age 16, I was able to buy my very first car. But the wealth I acquired because of showbiz inflated my ego. It also fooled me into believing I was invincible and could buy anything. With money came prestige. And then people, including my parents, started giving me special treatment which I used to my advantage. I felt—and lived—like a king. Or so I thought.

To the dismay of everyone around me, I began to develop a reputation for being a problematic actor.

ALCOHOLISM 101

I was exposed to alcohol at a very young age. The first time I got drunk was with an uncle. When I was about 10 or 11, after our taekwondo training, I would already have sips of alcohol. After doing well during practice, I would drink with teammates way older than me. We would go out to the streets and fool around, showing off our kicks. For instance, we would test one another if we could do a turning long kick even if we were drunk.

But as kids, we didn't know any better. We would all laugh and I thought it was a cool thing to do. It was like a passage into manhood. I brought this bad habit of mine when I entered showbiz. I wouldn't drink on set but I was only 13 or 14 when I would drink drinking at least four to five bottles every night. This went on for years and years until it became a very bad habit and escalated to other things such as drugs and sex with several women at a time. A debauchery kind of lifestyle. A part of my past that I am not proud of.

An experience with alcohol that I will never forget—-because it taught me a very important lesson—happened in Italy during the 65th Venice Film Festival.

I got so drunk during the after-party with those big-name Hollywood stars that I woke up at 6:20 a.m. the following day, not remembering anything and I realized I slept on a bench. Because of that, I missed my flight. I had to walk miles and miles to get to the water taxi and because I had no money, I jumped just as it was about to dock and ran as fast as I could. I had to walk for about two hours and then a Filipina saw me, brought me to the place where I was staying and lent me money for my fare. As a result of what happened, I lost an important film. A high price to pay for a wrong decision.

LOSING DAD AND MOM

As my career in showbiz prospered and I got more projects, I was also becoming a problem child not only at work but also at home. I started disrespecting my Mom. I learned to answer her back and offer all sorts of reasons to justify my actions. She would tell me that I was really smart because I could make red, blue and blue, red.

I was smoking a lot of marijuana and it was condoned. My mother couldn't do anything about it anymore.

I would buy a lot of weed which I would place in a backpack. I would bake space cakes, brownies laced with marijuana, and would even give them away to fellow actors and cameramen on the set.

Dad was already in pain during that time and smoking marijuana together became our bonding session. He used to tell me: "Hey son, roll me a joint. Bake me some brownies." Strangely, Dad and I got closer when he was dying. He eventually died of multiple organ failure.

It was when my father passed away that I lost my sense of direction and source of guidance. Donnie was always abroad because he had to compete as part of the Philippine Taekwondo Olympic Team. I used to blame him and tell him it was his fault that I turned out the way I did. Did he really expect me, the youngest in the family, to take care of Mom? It was his responsibility because he was the older brother. For the nth time, I turned to alcohol for comfort. And again, it was downward from there. It would take me a while to get out of that dark hole.

Another heartbreaking event would happen to me in 2017 when I lost my mom. She died of multiple sicknesses. I had to convince myself that Mom was in a better place, that she was already spared from the physical pain that she had to endure for several years. But in my heart, I know that I will aways feel deep pain and loneliness that she was already gone. She and I may have our misunderstandings and differences like all parents and children and we had to deal with difficult situations all throughout life but she will always be my anchor and my rock. I will forever be grateful for her love and kindness. My only regret was that she wasn't able to see me clean from addiction. But I will continue to keep her memories in my heart as I struggle and triumph through life with the intention of making her proud.

VISUAL ARTIST

A side of me that most people probably don't know about is that I am a self-taught visual artist and have participate in art exhibits already.

Painting was and still my outlet to express myself

I get a little emotional when I am asked about my paintings because I was able to finish more than a hundred works already but lost them all when our house got burned down in 2004.

It was my former sister-in-law who encouraged me to try my hand at painting. She gifted me with chalk, oil, pastel, and a book to get me started. I was self-taught, perfected my strokes and style and then moved to a different medium.

I told the press at that time that I went into painting to "conquer my demons." This was following a controversial mixed martial arts fight I had with an indie actor. It was also my way of taking my mind off alcohol while battling loneliness. Those were dark times so I turned to art to keep my head above water and to feel good about the world again. Art briefly became my cathartic escape.

In October 2017, my works were featured in the Smile With Us on World Smile Day event in Makati City. Organized by Smile Train Philippines, the exhibit was in recognition of the organization's partners and doctors that helped achieve their goal of improving the lives of Filipino children with cleft. Several of my paintings are with the Museo Ning Angeles in Angeles, Pampanga.

MEMORABLE PERFORMANCES

Throughout my career as an actor, spanning about 3 decades now, there have been several projects that I believe made a mark in the industry and also made me appreciate my craft more. In 2005, I won PMPC's Best Single Performance by an Actor for the Maalaala Mo Kaya episode entitled "Trolley."

Another unforgettable project of mine is the 2008 Cinemalaya entry, Jay where I portrayed Jay, a director-producer who is making a documentary on a brutally murdered teacher also named Jay. I won Best Actor for my role in the film, which was directed by the late Francis Xavier Pasion. I'm proud to say that I also co-produced the movie. In 2010, I won my second Best Actor award in Cinemalaya for the film, Donor, directed by Mark Meily. I portrayed the live-in partner of a woman who gets married to a sick foreigner so she could donate her kidney to him.

In 2017, I ventured into a relatively new territory and acted in a stage musical for the first time. I played Tikbalang in Tanghalang Pilipino's "Aurelio Sedisyoso" and won Outstanding Male Featured Performance in a Musical at the 2018 Gawad Buhay Awards.

On my Instagram account, I posted that my God never ceases to amaze me. I was in awe at being given the award. In fact, I was shocked and I felt that was not worthy of such a recognition. But my God keeps making me realize how I should start believing in myself, too. Perhaps that award was just one of the many countless ways that He reminded me to always recognize the talent He has given me, appreciate it more and to put it to good use all the time.

Another iconic role TV viewers will always remember me for is the character Dante "Bungo" Madarang in the long-running action series "FPJ's Ang Probinsyano." I played one of the villains to Coco Martin's Cardo Dalisay.

Although it was a role that showcased my acting prowess and the depths of my character's rage, I was somehow relieved that it was killed off seven months after I played it in the early part of 2019. The evilness of Bungo was getting into me and I had a hard time shaking it off. It also contradicted my being an ambassador for the Christian group I was a part of. However, I will forever be grateful to Coco

Martin for giving me the opportunity to be part of his very popular show.

Throughout my entire acting career, I will never forget the late actor-director Johnny Delgado, who I starred with in the ABS-CBN drama series, Calla Lily. He gave me the book "No Acting Please" by acting coach, Eric Morris. I consider Mr. Delgado my mentor as he taught me to correct my acting techniques and aim for authenticity when I portray a character. Beyond that, he was also that one person in the industry who made me feel respected and valued. What an honor it was to be treated that way by a fellow actor, a highly respected one at that. I will always be thankful to him for teaching me not only to be a better actor but most importantly, to be a better human being.

I've done so many roles, big or small, lead or a supporting one, protagonist or villain and I've always believed in the saying that there are no small roles, only small actors. My dream role? Juan Luna. I've read about him and he's a very interesting character. He's the brother of General Antonio Luna. He's hot-headed. He's an elitist. A great painter. I love his artworks. He put the Philippines' art scene on the international map when he won in Spain. I could identify with his idiosyncrasies, his paranoia. I think I will be able to do him justice if I play him in a movie. And I've always wanted to work on a project with award-winning director, Jerrold Tarog who did Heneral Luna and Goyo. I hope I could get to play Juan Luna with him directing me someday. I could also speak lines in Spanish and French if the role requires it. I already did a character who spoke Maguindanaoan.

I don't think there will ever be a time that I will quit acting. I love what I do. It's my life. As an actor, I am using this talent that God has given me.

MY MIRACLE

Now, let me tell you about my personal savior here on earth. She is my daughter, Talitha Cumi or Tali for short. She came to my life in January 2020 and instantly made me a doting father. I have always loved being around children and for a long time, I longed to have my own child. So, when I found out that I was going to be a father, I was elated. I was ready to embrace fatherhood. I prayed for it to happen.

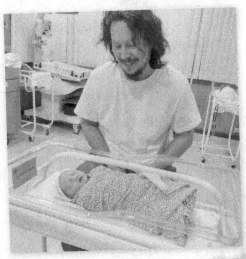

New born baby "Tali" born in 2020.

I spent an entire year with Sir Lyndon Angan teaching me about family. Above all, he taught me about how all-encompassing the Father's love is.

With good friend Lyndon Angan

Sure, there were also fears and doubts but I will always be thankful to the Lord for giving me this honor and privilege to raise such a beautiful and precious child. When I saw the ultrasound for the very first time, I couldn't help but shed tears of joy. I kept on crying that the doctor must have thought I was weird. But it was such a joyous moment. Something that I will remember for as long as I live.

While it has its challenges, having Tali in my life has given me immeasurable joy and motivation to do good and to always get back on my feet everytime I fall. Tali is my main reason for being, my sunshine, my source of pure joy. I am an overprotective father. I love her with all my heart and I am amazed every day witnessing her small milestones. I am in awe of her progress as she learns to navigate through life one adorable smile at a time. I believe she is also God's way of sending me a reassuring message during times of uncertainty as she is the most certain thing in my life right now.

Everytime I look at my daughter, I feel God's faithfulness even more as I am reminded by this Bible verse: "I prayed for this child, and the Lord has granted me what I asked of him." (1 Samuel 1:27)

OF FAME AND INFAMY

A Google search of my name would lead you to, among others, the many controversies I've figured in for the past several years. I was probably too clueless to realize the extent of my notoriety until I had an encounter years ago with a woman from Greece while I was at the Hong Kong Airport. I struck a conversation with her and we began enjoying each other's company, basically flirting and having a few drinks. I confidently told her I am an actor from the Philippines, hoping to impress her. I even challenged her to search my name on Google then left her to order more drinks and food. However, when I returned she suddenly became awkward, even scared. She then told me she had to leave. Only then did I realize she may have come across the stories about me being involved in sexual harassment charges. I blew my chances again.

During that trip, I also got myself into trouble. And missed my flight. Again. All because of my uncontrollable drunkenness. As a result, I lost another important project. I was supposed to play the lead in a Maalaala Mo Kaya special but was told I had already been replaced. Another lesson learned the hard way.

I regret that I had to go through all of these unfortunate incidents that hurt and disappointed a lot of people but I've accepted them all as an integral part of my journey towards forgiveness and healing. I've already made peace with most of the people I have wronged and offered apologies for what I have done to them.

In October 2017, I was detained in Lapu-Lapu City for smoking at a lavatory and I had to go to Cebu to pay fines or face imprisonment from six months to six years.

A friend of mine introduced me to Sir Jheck Yap of the Yap Wellness Center in Cebu City, where I sought temporary shelter. They were very patient and understanding with me, encouraging me to shape up and get serious with my rehabilitation. But I still went back to Pampanga.

Perhaps one of the lowest points of my life was when I was arrested in March 2018 for threatening my brother-in-law with a knife. That time, I felt that my family was ganging up on me and I was unable to hold my pent-up anger.

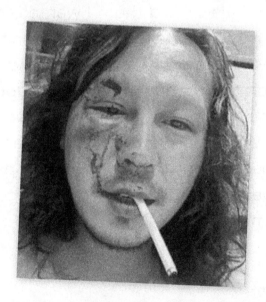

Police arrested me and I was detained at the Police Station 3 in Angeles, Pampanga then transferred to the Pampanga District Jail. I was locked up in a tiny cell next to a dirty toilet. It was during this time that I got a wake-up call from God again, one that made me reassess my life and my behavior. Whenever I recall all I went through during this distressing period in my life, this is the Bible verse, from Romans 3:23-24, that resonates with me: for all have sinned and fall short of the glory of God, and all are justified freely by his grace through the redemption that came by Christ Jesus."

My road to redemption started when my family visited me in jail. I told them I wanted to go back to Cebu and complete my rehabilitation for alcohol rehabilitation there. I really didn't know why but I guess I felt that Cebu would do me good. And it did. I've met a lot of good-hearted people, including mentors, rehab coaches and business partners, who have helped me turn my life around and persistently encouraged me to turn away from my vices without any judgment.

NEWFOUND HOME

Cebu has afforded me not just a change in pace and scenery but also the chance to harness my entrepreneurial skills. Away from the glaring lights and demands of showbiz, except the times when I have to leave to fulfill my work assignments, I have been able to partner with like-minded individuals in my business pursuits. In late 2018, I opened a barbershop. And in the early part of 2019, I was able to achieve my goal of launching an apparel line. Called Bungo Apparel, the collection's focal point in its designs is patterned after my long-haired character, Bungo.

In October 2021, I registered as a voter in the north district of Cebu City and encouraged Cebuanos to exercise their right to vote. I wanted to remind my fellow citizens that it is our sacred right to choose the leaders who will lead us based on their solid platform of governance and a set of moral values which will guide their decisions and actions towards the common good.

For the past four years, Cebu has been my refuge, my sanctuary, my home. Those years were very beautiful ... until super typhoon Odette struck in December 2021. Like everyone who went through the many challenges the storm brought, I had to hustle to look for water for the house, especially that I have a baby. I experienced having to wait in line for three hours just to get fuel. As a father, I had to prove that I could take care of my daughter.

I helped clear the streets from the debris, such as fallen tree trunks, that was left in the wake of the typhoon. It felt good to do good. But somehow it wasn't enough. My depression came back and I relapsed after the fifth day as I dealt with the trauma. I was able to fix myself before Christmas of 2021 because I had to prepare for a shoot in La Union.

My flight had to be moved to a later date because we couldn't book immediately due to poor Internet connection. My experience with Odette made me realize that even if you're a Christian, if you get rattled or demoralized by things you can't control such as a natural calamity or a tragedy, it's very easy to do things on my own without the guidance of Jesus. I realized that if you are a true Christian and you are in His presence, you have to wait for His signal before you start moving. But it was not Christ in me but Baron in me. And that's the reason why I failed.

LIFE RENEWED

Being part of Christ's Commission Fellowship, I continue to seek the Lord and fortify my relationships with people around me as I overcome my alcohol addiction. I am not embarrassed to admit that I am still a work in progress. I also deal with bipolarism and I am slowly getting back on track, processing things with my discipleship group.

As a born again Christian, I believe the Lord is not done with me yet. He is still writing my story. Or more accurately, He is guiding me as a pick up a pen and continue writing my own story.

I know a lot of people can identify with what my family and I have gone through, especially the struggles and challenges of living a Christian life.

I admit that at first I was ignorant about His Word. Yes, I read the Bible but I didn't really fully understand it. And in my three years in Cebu, I met a lot of people, who have helped me understand

God's Word by actually living it. Inspired by them, I continue to pray so that I may find my greater purpose, aside from being an actor and a father. That I may fully practice unconditional love, not the selfish kind. I am working on becoming my authentic self and knowing what is really important in my life. I just have to contented and appreciative of what I have while I continue with my spiritual journey and connect with those who are taking the same path. Even just one person with whom I can have a good conversation is very important to me.

I've also come to realize that achievements are temporary. God, loved ones, friends and family are more important and lasting. Selfishness will lead you to loneliness, despair and anxiety. It will lead you to hell. I will try my best not to go towards that path again. My aim now is to live a balanced life. And I have several people to thank for helping go through life amidst so many difficulties.

One of them is my spiritual father, Sir Lyndon, who has been selflessly been giving me valuable advice for years now. I call him Dad. He has never judged me, even when I was on relapse recently. In fact, when I was so depressed because of typhoon Odette and even if he doesn't like hanging out with me when I go on relapse, he let me be and even calmed me down instead of complaining about my life's issues. He always makes time for me. When I sought out his company, we just talked about life and God over good food. What I love about him is that he understands people. He is never self-righteous.

Sir Lyndon and I have known each other since I was 15 when I was one of the image models of a Cebu-based clothing company he was in charge of. We go a long way back and I am even a godfather to one of his children. All these years we've managed to keep in touch and he is one of those people who has never abandoned me despite my failings. Three months before I went into rehab in Pampanga, I called him and that's when he started visiting me every Saturday and Sunday. He would pick me up so I could join him and his family for the 9 a.m. Sunday worship at the Maranatha Christian Fellowship. And then he brought me to Dumaguete City to evangelize and do work for Make My Trip Travel TV.

After about six months, he encouraged me to ask God to open doors for me and after a few weeks, offers such as a film with director Brillante Mendoza came in, followed by my stint with FPJ's Ang Probinsyano. I will always be grateful to him. He has given me hope.

As an actor, I continue to grow as I take on different roles and projects that will enrich my experience and expand my portfolio. I consider myself among the fortunate ones to still be entrusted with film projects amidst the pandemic. One of these is the movie "Pusoy" which was produced by Viva Films and Cannes award-winning director Brillante Mendoza for Vivamax. I was also able to leave for Rotterdam, Netherlands in November 2021 to shoot a film that will be streamed on Netflix. Produced by Mavx Productions Inc., and directed by Marla Ancheta, the movie is about the bond between a father and his daughter, something that I can very well relate to.

I have learned to embrace the challenges of my profession and I constantly try my best to avoid triggers that will lead me to that dark path again. It hasn't been easy but I will never stop trying until I become that person the people I love will be proud of. When I am faced with difficulty, I turn to God who never fails to assure me: "The righteous cry out, and the Lord hears them; he delivers them from all their troubles." (Psalm 34:17)

MILESTONE ACHIEVED

I might have surprised people with the news that late in life, I was finally able to finish college. On April 25, 2022, I made it to the headlines again but this time and without no prior fanfare, it was for a good reason. I marched up the stage of All Nations College in Antipolo, Rizal to receive my diploma for completing my bachelor's degree in Theology. I am a proud member of the Batch 2021-2022 graduates. Unknown to many, I began my studies in Theology in the year 2019. Amidst the pandemic which halted the world in 2020, I went ahead with my studies with a dual purpose: achieve my goal and know my Savior more intimately. Throughout those trying and confusing times, I felt His all-encompassing presence as I struggled with my own personal demons.

It has always been a goal of mine to complete my studies but I am well aware that I wouldn't have been able to do it without the help and understanding of so many people who gave me the encouragement I needed to finish what I started. I thank the staff and administration of All Nations College for helping me accomplish my long-time goal. They assisted me in constructing a plan so that I could still study despite my hectic and oftentimes unpredictable schedule as an actor.

I am filled with joy at finally ticking this off my bucket list but also saddened because I know I will miss the discipline and routine my studies imposed on me. While this is a significant milestone in my life, I consider my college graduation as only the beginning of my continuing desire to be life's constant and consistent learner. I won't stop here. I hope to continue studying and acquiring more knowledge, if God wills it. And I want this personal achievement to serve as inspiration to everyone who dreams of finishing school. My life is a testament that it is never too late. God will work wonders in your life if you allow Him to guide you towards the right path.

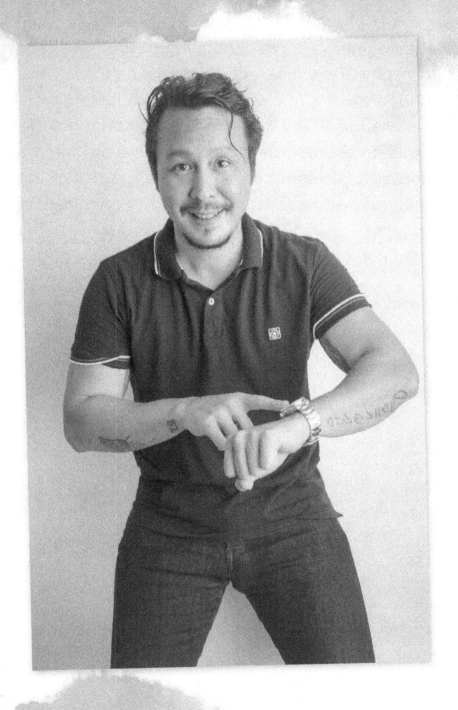

A testimony I shared at Maranatha Christian Fellowship in 2018 Cebu City, Philippines

Growing up, my father always compared me with my older brother and him being the naturally gifted athlete, my brother always excelled and I always came up short to our father's expectations.

Not until I started and was discovered as a child actor that I started to enjoy and have fun being in front of the camera and limelight.

And as I grew in the industry, film and movie projects came in, and of course, more projects mean more money and when there is more money, the pleasures of this world I became attached since it was at my disposal and I have the means for it.

The pleasures of the world included

- Drugs
- Sex
- Anxiety Attacks
- Pornography
- Self Medication
- Alcohol Abuse
- Depression
- and believe me a lot more

Little did I know during that time, I was headed to self destruction, the industry that i was in and has helped me achieve my dreams has made me turn into an angry man.

Angry if I don't get what I want
Angry with everyone

But most of all

I was angry with myself since I felt I don't know who I am anymore.

Everyone, I felt in the industry, with media, friends, and family I need to please them, indeed to perform for them, I practically was lost who I was.

And believe me, being an actor, I was good in faking it.

So in turn, my only outlet was booze, sex and lust to make me feel good even for a short span of time.

For years, because of all the booze, almost lost count of how many times it was in rehab and spending prison time.

And yes, with all these strongholds of what I got entangled myself into, I did try not just once but a couple more times to end my life, I wanted it, but He never wanted it to happen.

And this brings me to the reason why I am up here, not to share about myself
But...
Sharing with you of what He has done and what He is still going to do

In Galatians: 4 : 7
You are no longer a slave, you
are now a child of God

That promise, I lay claim from a person that has lost his identity, He restored who I was not in the eyes of men, but the way He sees me.
The first time, I got connected with you in faith and the Men's Ministry of this church, I was not condemned at all, and I am most encouraged when I met Pastor Joe Disarno for the very first time and he knew why I was here and I remembered him saying "son, we are not here to condemn you but to show you His goodness because of the Cross" ,

of course, I did not understand it at that time, but the church and the men's ministry has pointed me to that direction and will forever be grateful for that.

In Galatians 2:20
You are not defined by your past

I know being in the limelight for so long, easily the world could pass up judgement and the downside of it, is how bad and wild i am.

I am aware that I have a long way to go
I have broken relationships
I have dishonored and disrespected people
I have carried and endured hurts and pain

But

I am encouraged, that His word is true, that as I continue to discover Him everyday, one day and at His ordained time and place, reconciliation and restoration will soon come to pass.
And lastly,

Galatians 5 : 25
Don't be led by feeling and
emotions, be led by the Holy Spirit

I thank God for this church and the men's ministry, for showing me the gifts and fruit of the Holy Spirit. Never did I experience so much intimacy and personal encounter that transformed my outward self and be transformed from the inside and out.

I have a long way to go and I pray that, just as you heard my story, it is no longer my story, but His story of finding that one and leaving the 99 and that one happens to be me.

Thank you and to God be all the Glory

*Inside the Main Sanctuary of Maranatha
Christian Fellowship Cebu City, Philippines*

CPSIA information can be obtained
at www.ICGtesting.com
Printed in the USA
LVHW050707080523
746320LV00002B/316